# An Indigo Child's Journey to Loving Herself

*River Russell*

Order this book online at www.trafford.com
or email orders@trafford.com

Most Trafford titles are also available at major online book retailers.

Printed in the United States of America.

ISBN: 978-1-4269-9732-7 (sc)
ISBN: 978-1-4269-9733-4 (e)

*Trafford rev. 02/15/2012*

 www.trafford.com

**North America & international**
toll-free: 1 888 232 4444 (USA & Canada)
phone: 250 383 6864 ♦ fax: 812 355 4082

# What is an Indigo Child?

For most of an Indigo Child's life, they go unrecognized and unappreciated. He/she may feel scorned for who she is—without even fully knowing why. Indigo Children can be very emotional and sensitive to the energy around them. They are typically diagnosed with mental conditions such as ADHD, ADD, etc; however, these are not necessarily bad "conditions." Indigo Children typically exhibit extraordinary talent in the arts (music, drawing, painting, etc.), technology-related activities, or sometimes in athletic activities.

Indigo Children are very good at understanding people and communicating with them. They can be described as "old souls" and they themselves may not fully understand their own life purpose—and what they want to accomplish on this Earth. If you are interested in finding more, I strongly recommend reading *Indigo Children: The New Kids Have Arrived* by Lee Carroll.

*Note:* As you begin to read this story, please note that some names have been changed to protect the character's privacy. This is a true story.

# *Purpose*

I chose to write this book, because after working with many youth and interacting with even people older than me—I have realized that many people think that love (from someone else) will fill them even when people let them down. It is almost like the Western World really prepares children to think this—and we go seeking love throughout our lives—in this kind of way, and we become very disappointed with others and ourselves. We walk down a road we don't have to walk down. Unfortunately, some people don't come out of that walkway alive.

I hope that this book can teach people that THERE IS another way to live and that THERE IS another way to love-yourself and others. I hope that this book will soothe the point at wherever you are in life now (whether it is a point of suffering or perhaps just curiosity/questioning). I welcome you into my heart in this book, and I am trusting you with it. May this book bring you strength, wisdom, and most of all—love for who you are.

Gravity pulled my body down on the small wooden chair. "Close your eyes," her voice rang like a crystal. Where was she taking me? "Now, think about all the love you had for Jackie." I thought about all the times we brushed our teeth together, cuddled, and just drove aimlessly in her car for what seemed like decades. The images continued as Laura said, "Now, capture all the love you had for Jackie and give it to yourself . . ."

Jackie was probably somewhere else, right now, eyeing the girl she lived with. My mind collected all the love, pulling it down to my abdomen and trying to send it to my heart. "Open your eyes," Laura said. I opened them and Laura presented a mirror in front of me. Her voice rang softer, "Now, give yourself the love that you had for Jackie. Look into the mirror and say, 'I love you.'"

I looked at Laura, smiled, and raised my eyebrows. I looked into the mirror and saw my soft, deep brown eyes, my short chopped thick hair complimenting my firm jaw and high cheekbones. I smiled. I really was beautiful. Laura watched me as I looked at myself. "I love you." The words came out fast and with a giggle. Laura caught my eyes, and smiled with me. She understood this was new for me. I tried again, "I love you." I kept repeating the same lines with a little more confidence each time and blushing a little less.

Each time, I looked in the mirror, I saw more of my emotion: the way my smile just came alive. I saw the way my eyes showed every emotion, and were so open with everyone—even myself and Laura. Laura and I had met with each other two times previously; and here, I was sitting in this small wooden chair, and I felt like she understood me more than anyone I had met in my whole life—even more than my parents and my best friends.

Laura ended my session by softly looking into my eyes. Her eyes were a miraculous blue, vibrating constantly, teeming with life—like the universe. I couldn't stare into her eyes too long, without feeling nervous and excited. I didn't know what that meant, but I did know that I loved looking into her eyes. Laura's eyes were full of hope, love, faith, and energy for everything we humans stood for; it was amazing to me that I could know and talk to another sensitive, believing, open individual. At that moment in my life, Laura was beautiful to me.

Laura's words stuck with me after that session. I wanted a relationship deeply in my heart; I had grown to not miss Jackie, but I had grown to miss the quality time and connection a relationship could enhance in one's life. Laura said wisely, "You know what're you're looking for, River?" You know what you're looking for? You are the one you're looking for. You are your own partner."

I kind of looked at her strangely and smiled openly. I kind of laughed—thinking she was kidding at first. She was still holding the mirror in front of me. Laura was right! "That's interesting . . ." She could tell I was speechless and feeling what she was saying within me.

As I sit and write this, I am a long way from where I was one year ago—sixth months ago—even three months ago. Time is no indicator of health, of where your heart is, of where you are and what you are seeking. Time will always be moving; emotional and spiritual health is about how much you choose to put into it—just like school, but the rewards are so much more fulfilling and lasting. You receive the reward of knowing yourself and what you are really seeking in your life.

I am going to take you on a journey. A long, winding journey that is engraved in my heart and can never be wiped away; I have grown to cherish this, no matter how painful this journey was for me. I encourage you to get comfortable and to open your heart, as we make this journey together. My intentions of writing this book are to define love—a real love, that members of our society are unawakened by—a love that is so strong, that it can kill—if we, as individuals, aren't grounded and prepared for where it takes us in life.

My story starts in a little town called Worton, Maryland where I was completing my internship through Indiana University at Echo Hill Outdoor School. I had been living among many intellectuals; we were all Teachers together and I knew I wasn't quite in the right place. As Outdoor Teachers, we would spend our days with students from 8 am to 9 at night, sometimes being a host in a rustic tent with them. On my weekends, I spent much time alone—sleeping, writing, and reading. I think I was trying to understand who I was contrasted by many different people. After my internship, I started working at a wonderful Quaker camp in Vermont called Farm and Wilderness.

Towards the end of my internship, I started sending messages to a young woman, named Jackie. At Indiana University (IU), I had seen her in and out of the dormitory's dinig hall where I worked. She was just a freshman and I was a senior, ready to get out in the world. I was pretty sure she was gay, but I was so scared to talk to her. She was on the rugby team and I knew in my mind—that she was probably young emotionally; also, she walked around like she owned the place. Why try and talk to her? Underneath it all, I was very scared. I couldn't get past her striking blonde hair, strong nose, and puffy red lips.

Sixth months later, I found myself messaging her. My friend from elementary school lived near her; this seemed like the perfect excuse to message her. Our messages fired back every few days—we had found common ground with an affinity for Mother Nature, women, spirituality, and hard work. My heart smiled when she wrote at the end of a message, "Peace and love." This woman continued to intrigue me.

Over the next two months, our messages grew deeper and deeper. Upon making my first phone call to Jackie and hearing her voice and her peace with water while kayaking, I found myself telling her that, "I loved her" and yet we had not met yet. I had just rode my first train from Maryland to Vermont. Right after those words were released, the Farm and Wilderness van arrived to pick me up. Saying goodbye on the phone and returning to a Quaker land, where I would have to use a landline—already seemed to be a challenge for me. And yet the green mountains and Vermont fresh air were glimmering around me; at this moment in time, this somehow was not enough for me.

Vermont is a beautiful land. I continued my professional life as I went from being an Outdoor Teacher to a Camp Counselor for my nine and ten year olds; they require a lot of energy. I went through a week of staff training and couldn't believe the kids were arriving in a few days. I had spent several nights video chatting with Jackie and there were very few moments that I didn't stop thinking about her. It was weird how I had never officially met this young woman, but I was falling in love.

Jackie wanted to visit, but I thought it would be too much money and she should wait till I would return to Indiana. It was a sensible thought, but she insisted that she came and visit. We made the plans. I took off two days, she made travel plans—and we waited. Well, we really anticipated—our video chat sessions only seemed to keep getting longer and more frequent. I felt out of space at Farm and Wilderness and I was not getting enough sleep.

I left for a three-day backpacking trip with my nine and ten year old campers and I pulled my lower back. I was in a great amount of pain. My days suddenly became hard, challenging, and almost like tests of my patience. Small things infuriated me. I found my patience and tolerance with my campers and co-workers had severely diminished; these qualities were not reflective of my usual qualities.

The truth was that I had been working with children consistently for nearly four months—with not enough time to care for my inner self; and now, it was tearing on me physically. The time before Jackie arrived flew by—I picked her up, and our weekend felt like a fairy tale. We stayed in a three-sided cabin in the middle of the woods in southeasten Vermont.

The weekend is captured by green trees everywhere, her wonderful smile, watching her cook over a fire, sipping beer, holding each other, and being in awe of the mountains in Vermont; we couldn't separate our lips from each other. We smelled of bacon, fire, and fresh rain. I wrote this poem, following that weekend:

when my spirit stands up tall to defend itself,
she rocks me back and forth,
with her soothing words,
her graceful grounded spirit.
when my back flares up to resist work,

her strong hands press the exact location
to take me on a physical vacation.
i'm longing to feel her hands again.

every interaction, every exchange of eye contact,
every touch
expresseses her unconditional love,
her support, her acceptance, of me
that i haven't fully felt
since my father lived.

unconditional love seemed a dying language
no one spoke or wanted to speak anymore,
but i am so glad to share
that i can feel her unconditional love
from this far away.

I wrote many more poems (some of which, I may share here). Her departure from Vermont was hard—she cried, she cried so deeply. I was holding her softly and firmly, telling her all would be okay; I would be near soon. Her tears were wet and so alive—they didn't stop flowing. She kissed me deeply and so passionately in front of strangers, right there in rural Vermont. That was the first time I had kissed a woman so fully and openly, in public. Her tears still ran during our kisses. I could feel her fear of losing me.

She walked away like a stone soldier. I knew that I would see her again. I returned to Bloomington one week later. It was time for me to take care of myself. My back was aching me—it was hard to sleep and my pain was not getting any better. I refused to go to a doctor while in Vermont.

What could a doctor do? I knew I needed relaxation. The noises from my campers were so loud sometimes—I felt my back flare every time I heard a yell. It was time to take care of me or that was my intention.

I returned to Bloomington to be with Jackie. She was elated and shocked. I told her I wouldn't stay long and that I would indeed return home. This was the beginning of our relationship—this is where Jackie and I officially began our time together—in a small apartment of hers in Bloomington, Indiana with other roommates.

We started our relationship off awkwardly. I remember she talked about her clothes for the first two hours! I remember her mumbling how nervous she was about having me there. My compassionate heart was so open and yet so overwhelmed about being there. How could I judge her for talking about her clothes?

She took me out on several dates to the organic restaurant she worked at. We went on walks; we cuddled together, watched some movies, and had deep conversations. I learned more about Jackie and her ways of life. She had been with many partners and she was several years younger than me; this intimidated me and I felt violated, as a sensitive person. I couldn't help but wonder if she still loved them.

When Jackie worked, I found myself writing, swimming, doing yoga, and sleeping to heal my back. I was doing the right things for myself. Sometimes, I hated being away from her, because I really did enjoy spending time with her.

When we decided we were serious, I started researching cars (I didn't own a car at the time), a place to live, and an available job; it was so much to take on with the current economy, but I was dedicated to her and myself.

Our first conflict occurred when I met one of her deep ex-girlfriends who was transitioning. They talked about sex like it was a transaction; my heart felt dirty, washed away by a hurricane that night. I was quiet the whole night and I could not relate to this friend of hers. He talked about himself the entire night. For a brief while, I really wondered who Jackie was.

This should have been an unhealthy indicator for me, but my compassionate heart moved, moved like a soft river. We are all growing individuals. Jackie sensed I was irritated by something. At the time I couldn't put it into words. I remember reading my book—and wanting desperately to be alone. We went for a walk and changed the subject (she had asked to come on the walk).

She didn't like to see me so tense about my future—especially if I wanted to be with her. I kept an Excel sheet of all the jobs I had applied for. I took a significant loan from my parents so that I could live independently from them. I had even debated on moving home, but my parents weren't too excited about that. I needed a job, but it was proving hard. I spent most of August online researching for jobs, sleeping, writing, and praying when I wasn't with Jackie.

Jackie worked about 32 hours a week. She also kept herself busy with things like organizing her items, studying for summer school, and spending time with her friends (she is an extrovert). Soon, Jackie was to start school and I knew her world would become even busier. We both feared her start to school, because it would mean we would have even less time together. Jackie wanted me to meet one of her bosses—someone else she had slept with. The night she asked, I couldn't bring myself to go. Why would I want to meet this person? She said they were just friends, and she couldn't quite understand why I felt the way I did.

Jackie started school. I started working for a corporation third-shift in September. Our lives changed deeply from this moment forward. She was mad that I took a job working third-shift, but I trusted that she understood this is what kept me in Bloomington, near her. I really loved Jackie. Working for a corporation killed a small part of me—I worked when everyone slept. I worked underneath bright lights, moving boxes, and amongst people who were really about half as alive as myself. My boss was very demanding and harsh with me, because he knew I could work hard. Most of my staff members were negative; and yet, I noticed they gravitated to my smile.

As time continued, I was given more responsibility by leading the health and beauty section (organizing items by aisle) and by unloading the back stock items on the line— single handly by myself. By the last week of my time there, my lats were so huge that when I wore a shirt—you could see them. This gives you an idea of how heavy these back stock items were. I would sweat so much at work—that I could hardly ever eat during my shifts (and rarely ate during the day as time wore on).

Throughout my time, I continued to search for other work—even minimum wage work. I desperately wanted another job. I knew that the corporation was taxing on me; but, I also realized I had my own free time. This was nice. I was able to go to Barnes and Noble and read and write for hours upon time without camper's echoes nearby. I love my silence and quiet time.

Jackie and I found our moments to spend time together, but it became challenging. We started to plan our dates primarily because she was so busy. My third-shift lifestyle wasn't very convenient for her. I would spend the nights at her dorm. I specifically bought a special parking pass even though I was no longer a student. I could park right outside her dorm.

I remember calling her at 7am, to let me into her dorm. Her sleepy eyes, and spiky blonde hair always made me smile. No matter how hard my day was, I was always elated to see her. She was my special girl. I would shower, and usually unwind from work by writing or something. Then, I would join her in bed, cuddle, and sleep—until the afternoon. I would sometimes awake and eat lunch with her. And, then enjoy dinner with her. This is how our days were usually spent, because my lifestyle was different from hers. We went on a date every two weeks or so.

While the sex we had was grand, I enjoyed cuddling with her the most. I felt like we were one at times—and there was no better feeling in the world, for me:

> her body next to mine
> the Earth seems to spin slower and slower
> because she's cuddled inside my arms,
> our eyes close
> bodies join: our lungs create a rhythm.
> my heart can finally rest on this Earth,
> there are no pockets between us,
> our spirits are feeling peace together.
> the Earth seems to spin slower and slower.
> i love being next to her.

As each month went by, I generally gave her a rose and a poem. She loved it so much that she started to look forward to it. Looking back, it is quite ironic, because as much as we both loved the outdoors, Jackie and I only did two outdoor activities together:

1) We went to an apple orchard (and didn't pick apples)
2) We went camping once—in which she did homework.

Love is a beautiful emotion—it can surpass all evils. I really do believe it can. I loved Jackie so much—to infinite means. Jackie has pages and pages of poetry I wrote her; at one time, I demanded them back. She reluctantly gave them back to me, after much prodding. For awhile, I reread them when I was hurting deeply to understand how I loved her. I believe that love will bring us to a greater vibration of harmony, peace, and tranquility on this Earth—if we believe and follow this feeling within ourselves and others.

There wasn't a week that went by that I did not write her a poem. When I worked and I heard a song about love, she was in my heart. When I became tired at work, I would remember how hard Jackie worked—and motivate myself to continue. I reminded myself of how blessed I was to be in Bloomington, near Jackie. I respected her desire to work hard and succeed, but I also reminded Jackie to remember herself and to care of herself. I am not sure if she understands that fully to this day.

I wanted Jackie to walk a path of spirituality with me. And, I don't think I fully knew that when I was in a relationship with her. I remember on one of my days off, I went to a park near my house, and I walked around to feel the Divine's presence. I felt calm and somewhat centered afterwards. After getting into my car, I saw a couple walking into the park together; there weren't many people there. I remember crying to Jackie days later about how I wanted to do more meaningful, deep activities together—like walking in a park and sharing nature. I felt alone during that moment at the park.

This was at about our six month anniversary together; from there, the conflict continued. The memories are very painful to recall. I remember having endless conversations with her about how I wanted to spend time outside with her—a bit more than a date every other week. She understood, but her actions weren't speaking the same language. I grew restless, tired, anxious, and impatient; this was not my usual self (and she told me that many times). When the holidays approached, she planned a snowboarding trip. She would be working and or gone for the holidays throughout her winter break. We had very little time together.

I worked Christmas Eve morning and New Year's Eve. I drove home during a snowstorm on Christmas Eve night. I remember not being able to sleep at all that night, because I thought I would die on the way back and that I would never see Jackie again. Obviously, I have a mild anxiety of driving, especially in hazardous weather.

Jackie returned from her snowboarding trip the first week of January. She would start school almost immediately. Deep down inside, I was scared I was losing her. Internally, my heart hurt so much already. I didn't realize this at the time. Our energies were different in the car ride home; she changed the station instantly, critiqued my driving, and talked fully of her own adventures. I listened, but I was so distant inside.

I asked myself inside, "What about my adventures? What about my work? What about how I missed her?" That week grew to be the hardest week of my life—because, spiritually, we had lost each other. I remember her telling me she felt that one day while at work, her whole heart felt completely empty "like I ran away." Tears erupt from my pores while I write this, because I was there—in Bloomington; I was so present for her. Before she left for snowboarding, I remember drawing one of my first sketches of her face. I wanted to remember her, I wanted to have her as close as I could while she was physically away.

I was really going to miss her. This was the first of many drawings that I would be making, later in my life— unbeknownst to me. (I did not think of myself as an artist whatsoever during this time.)

We really tried to bring our relationship to life—she and I enjoyed a few moments at my house by drinking wine, cooking, and bathing together. I loved taking baths with her. She usually said "no", but she knew how much it meant to me—when we were able to sit in the darkness together, in water—holding each other.

I wanted to make love to Jackie in the bathtub; she proceeded to tell me that this was dangerous and wouldn't work! After much pleading and asking, she finally agreed. I brought her to a magnificent orgasm and I lived for this! My heart was in so much joy, because I brought her a beautiful gift. In my heart, I felt we were doing okay.

I had a day off the next day, but for some reason—we did not spend time together. I remember being hurt and falling into my own world while reading Rudolf Steiner's work about love. There is a part that speaks about when we are in complete devotion to something/someone, that our body language depicts that. Images of Jackie and I rang prevalent in my mind's eye of our special moment in the bathtub together. I felt soothed and comforted by what I read and remembered. In my heart, I felt Jackie and I were going to be okay.

Jackie stopped by my apartment; I was leaving for work in a matter of ten minutes. She wanted to know what I was reading. Her heart was silent—*open*; she hadn't been like this for a long time. She had gone climbing and she was very grounded from her activity. I read Rudolf Steiner's touching words to her; she said that she could understand "only so much." I later drew her a picture of our lovemaking with the prose on the front of the page. I'm not sure if she understands to this day what Rudolf Steiner and I understand so well— the meaning of unconditional love.

The days that followed grew worse. I was upset for nearly being late to work, for her not being able to understand a philosopher and educator who at the time, was groundbreaking to me (and still means much to me to this day). I was upset that she could not find a convenient time to talk with me. It was like, during those dark dark cold days, I was finally understanding how she was treating me. The whole nine months we were together, I was finally seeing her reflection (and not my own): her harsh tone, her motivation to push herself beyond reality, her closed heart, her care for herself always overriding my own existence, her lack of sensitivity, her sexual past, and how afraid she was of herself.

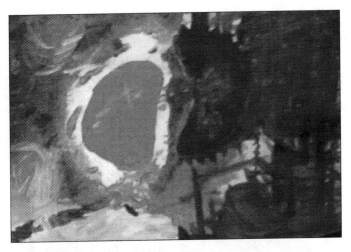

I saw all of these qualities and actions wrapped up in one ball; and yet oddly enough, I still did not want to lose her. Love was something I cultivated so easily as a child. I remember watching my own grown father cry. It is very natural for me to feel and cry and love—to experience emotions fully and deeply.

One particular Friday night, I wanted to speak with her—to talk like adults. She texted me that she had been "drinking and probably wasn't in a good space to talk." I desperately and deeply needed to talk. I remember parking right outside of her workplace—hoping, waiting, like I had done so many times. She called; she reported matter-of-factly that she would not be able to come out and talk.

There were voices in the background. Dozens of voices, loud music, and she was underage.

"Those voices were more important to her than me;" I remember thinking exactly that during that moment. I could not go home. I had just gotten a new job and she was giving up. I went to a close spiritual friend's house that night who held me, talked to me, and listened to me. Jackie gave up on me that night—as a friend, and as a lover. My heart hurt very deeply. My heart had never hurt so much in my life. It is a night that I do not prefer to remember, but alas it is a part of the journey.

I remember eating—and puking. I remember crying so hard and not being able to go to sleep. I remember feeling like a dagger had been stuck inside my abs—for the pure fun of it by Jackie. Her face burned in my heart, in a horrible way now. Why did I love her so much—if this was how she treated me?

In the past, I may have said it was not an abusive relationship. Even though we never had physical conflict, Jackie's words and her actions were very harmful to my soft, big, sensitive heart. She hurt me so deeply at that point in time, I felt that I would not awake in the morning.

The days that passed, passed. I cried some days. I felt nothing other days. I would go to Barnes and Noble and write poetry for multiple hours—about our past. These reflections help me see her reflection as separate from my own. I grew to say she was a "bitch" and to understand it was good we were not together (this took time). I sought counseling. I began a normal lifestyle of working during the daylight hours.

I started painting and drawing more. I ate more meals; before, I had been struggling to eat and it was unusual for me to vomit several times a week. I started weight lifting. I realized it was a great thing she was no longer in my life. I took better care of myself. Occasionally, I went to church. I kept researching bigger and better jobs to utilize my college degree. I went outside and played. I took long walks and talked to God. I spent time with friends. I sought my spiritual friends as well. I went to the gay bar while staying sober and danced numerous hours to feel myself come alive. I talked to strangers. I asked girls out. And yes, I got hurt over again—and again.

I went home and talked with my brothers. They told me they saw the negative impression Sarah had—but they were too humble to speak up. I was surprised. I demanded more honesty from my brothers.

I listened to music. I kept painting. I kept writing. I unexpectedly landed a salaried job an hour away from Bloomington. My mother told me "that it may not be the best fit," but I took yet another leap of faith. I knew intuitively that it was a good fit for me and it would challenge me to grow in ways that I needed to.

I moved into my own place less than a month later. It was going to be hard to leave Bloomington. I found myself among small, simplistic people—fitting right in (in this way). I cut my hair not too long after—and stuck out as either a boy or a dyke to people! I learned to no longer care what others thought about my physical appearance.

I found the joys and challenges of giving a part of my heart to my students. I found my natural connection as a leader again and developing long-term relationships with my students—to watch them grow and to see the life inside them (they may not know they had).

My paintings and poetry became deeper. I started sleeping better at night; sometimes, it was hard to get out of bed. I cooked for myself, enjoyed working out, and watched movies during my free time! I found myself loving my free time without a whisper of another human nearby. I found that I was getting to know myself even better—beyond a complicated-Jackie being nearby.

I painted several murals at my workplace in the weight room; the energy that came lasted for days! Wow! I realized what I was capable of—and am still to this day, in complete awe of my own talents. At that time, I knew I had a gift, but I needed to cultivate it more.

At that point in time, I sought spiritual guidance from an incredible person named Laura. I discovered the chakras again, spiritual energy, and my own limitations/perceptions. From time to time, I still do indeed cry over Jackie. I mentioned love before I began my story about Jackie. You have been through the motions and emotions of what I went through with Jackie. As a beginning spiritual sensitive individual, I am more likely to feel other's pain, to care deeply for others beyond my own self, and to even forget my own self.

If you are not sensitive or very emotional, this may not make much sense to you; however, if you are, you may be able to relate. I highly recommend reading about Indigo Children if you are sensitive in any way. We are entering a new spiritual time where New Energy is arriving, and we are bringing hope, kindness, and love to many humans who are living in this external, linear world.

My relationship ended with Jackie, because she failed to appreciate the deeper, inner qualities of myself so often that I became deeply hurt. I am not saying that a healthy relationship is one where we see someone daily or frequently, but a healthy relationship is ideally one where both individuals give and receive equally. I believe that there are many unhealthy relationships out there, because many humans look to fill themselves externally through their partner.

I think this approach will only lead to a dead-end in a relationship or a dead-ended within one's self where hopefully, someday soon—growth can endure. I have many beautiful memories that are carved into my heart with Jackie. Honestly, I don't remember many of them, because of how our relationship ended. While she did say, "I love you," to me often, her actions spoke a very different tone (as mentioned earlier in the book).

She would say to me sometimes, "I don't understand how you love me so deeply." I wrote this poem for her about a month before we ended our relationship:

*(Note: we shared William Blake's poem with each other often.)*

"To see a world in a Grain of Sand
And Heaven in a Wild Flower,
Hold Infinity in the palm of your hand
and Eternity in one hour." (William Blake)

To Hold a Heart in your open palm,
To see Heaven in a Wild Flower,
Your Heart is the Wild Flower
That I still Hold close to my own.

To see the Wild Flower open and close,
To feel the warm sun together,
To feel the brisk wind hit our cheeks,
I want to grow warm with you.

Holding your Wild Flower in my palm
is the most beautiful gift (I have ever received)
And I promise
to Hold you more softly, to look at you,
to listen deeper, to talk more softly,

and celebrate the creative moments that open,
not to destroy.
Uplift, dance, laugh
love, listen

You
My Wild Flower!!
Wild Flowers from different fields,

Let's dance together
And understand each other
All the more!!

My Wild Flower,
Mouth to touch
Touch to mouth
brings heart to heart.
Translation becomes innate this way quickly,
why does the wind feel so much warmer?

our Wild Flowers burn from here on out,
warmth against the freezing rain and frostbitten world,
shining during each moment,
our fields become one
slowly.

your roots embrace the ground
and grace others near you,
calming.

my petals watch the sky
and aim to see Heaven
in every smile and cry.
your roots pull me down beautifully,

feeding me—nourishing
my very core
that someone tore, a very long time ago,
with each touch, i heal.
my petals soften your core,
opening a little bit more than before.
with these words, with my mouth,
my sound waves may massage or poke
your beautifuly, strong Human Heart.

without roots, you cannot grow a flower.
without petals, the flower would not exist.
without water, how would a Wild Flower grow?

without sun, would the petals of a Wild Flower, long to open?
without nourishment and care, how would Wild Flowers grow?

how would Wild Flowers truly see each other
and long to dance and be merry, with another
without nourishment and care?

To see a World in the parts of a Wild Flower:
roots, petals, water, sun,
nourishment and care.
my petals see Heaven,
but how does Heaven, happen, here?

your roots decrease the fear
and allow me to see the
image in the mirror,
Heaven here.

petal and root together,
peacefully,
my heart fills fully
like sitting in a field of wild yellow flowers
waving together, warm sun heating me up,
the flowers tingle my heart,
breathing is our clock,
my heart fills fully
when i am with you, Wild Flower.

My Wild Flower,
Mouth to touch,
Touch to mouth
Brings roots to petals,
This will strengthen our stem.
Wild Flowers from different fields,
My Wild Flower!!,
Will you keep dancing with me?
We are Heaven together.

I remember watching Jackie and hearing her say, "I feel I'm not good enough for you." It broke my heart to hear her say that. And yet, there she was sitting, amidst my poetry-filled walls, crying so openly.

I cried too, because I could feel how much she was hurting. I looked into her eyes and said, "I love you Jackie. I love you for who you are—whether you're tired, hurting, or sad. It doesn't matter. You are enough. I love you baby." My tears filled my eyes. During that moment, I felt that we would never break up. During that moment, I had given her complete unconditional acceptance and love.

Jackie and I did not work because we were incompatible in terms of our personalities. We did not work because Jackie and I were too attached to each other; we needed to work on ourselves. Since our breakup, Jackie has been dating several people—and those are her choices she is free to make in her life. I have tried dating, but forced things too much—and not accepted the lack of chemistry/desire to be friends among women.

Seven months of being single has been hard and yet so blissful. I can nearly bench my weight. I am getting closer and closer to a six pack every day. I hope to have my student loans paid off in two years—or so. I am feeding young student's souls every day. I am able to create art and write poetry. And now, I am entering the gifts of my own sensitive, spiritual soul with joy and acceptance.

I am learning to say "no" to others to say "yes" to me— to build a better, healthier me. A fulfilled me. And not an empty vessel walking around aimlessly for false fulfillment. I am deciding what I want to do with my light and my life with each day.

Sometimes, other's ask, "Are you alone?"

"I am alone," I tell them, "And I love it."

They proceed to ask, "But, don't you feel alone?"

I smile inside and look them in the eyes, "I love myself." They don't fully understand and sometimes give me a puzzled look, but I cannot tell an individual the pathway to loving themselves.

I love my body, I love my mind, I love the way I am able to look at life—and the events and people who come into my life. I do have to be careful with people, because I am able to love others so deeply with ease. Sometimes, it is good for me to have distance from others; especially right now, because I am loving myself deeper and deeper with each day. Here are some examples in ways that I build a relationship with myself ("focusing on me"):

> I look in the mirror, and say, "I love you."
> I care for my body by working out, drinking more water, less caffeine, and eating when hungry.
> I am slowly getting into swimming and yoga—which is more healthy for my muscles than lifting.
> I am doing more meditation and grounding techniques.
> I am giving less to others and more to myself, to ensure that I am not running away from myself and seeking fulfillment in an unhealthy way.
> I am slowing my days down by doing the activities I deeply want to do.
> I allow myself to cry without judgment. (Looking in a mirror helps.)

The hardest obstacle for me was to overcome my desire of having someone close to me, beyond the world of sexual interactions. Masturbation, artwork, and writing are very meaningful forms of creation for me! My body was not made for casual sex; it would take a very special person and even then, I am not sure. Making love is a very deep spiritual, emotional connection for me—and why would I ever want to discolor that or dishonor my body?

I found that I missed cuddling the most—cuddling with Jackie. When Jackie's heart was softened at the end of the night, she loved it when I would hold her—my hand on top of her heart, or my hand in hers. Sometimes, I felt our dreams came together during the night—that we were one. I had to accept that Jackie and I were over, no matter how much I missed cuddling.

By being alone, I have learned that we send our reflections everywhere. ***People give us what we give them—whether it is good or bad or unclassifiable***. Upon realizing this, I finally asked myself, "Why did Jackie feel so comfortable cuddling with me (as she can be very guarded)?" And this is the answer that I arose to:

> trees dancing,
> I don't know where she is,
> but I'm in my bed
>
> breathing, beautifully,
> heart beating softly
> for me, for me.
>
> the images before us,
> can be a reflection of us-
> we just can't lose
> the deepest part of ourselves.
>
> my soft snowflake flannel sheets
> never fit so well in the summertime,
> i rest peacefully, for me
> today, because i can breathe and be
>
> love still flows

# *Conclusion*

As sensitive individuals/Indigo Children, we will find that we do reach out to others and heal their pain before our own. It is an activity that we are naturally wanting to do—unless we are mentored by our parents, teachers, and role models to not do so. It is a wonderful, natural gift to love and to give. And, it is so rewarding to see how we can make other people feel better! Why would we not want to use such a powerful, amazing gift?

It is important to remember however—that our gift will only be to our demise if we do not care for ourselves first; because if we care so much for others, eventually, we will indeed be hurt—if we have not first learned to love ourselves first.

These are lessons Indigo Souls must learn deeply—not just on an external level, but spiritually. Yoga and spiritual guidance have proved to be very healing and nurturing for me. I also find that quiet spaces, time in nature, and alone time are all that I need. I exercise early in the day to release my physical energy. I still have energy after this, but it is more creative energy that I can release.

When an Indigo Child is ready or of the appropriate age, Indigo children can learn and be guided by other sensitives that have gifts—that can help humanity with wisdom and knowledge. I think it is important for Indigo Children to have an older mentor who lives a healthy lifestyle in their life—in some way. This will help the Indigo Child know that it IS indeed possible to be themselves and to be happy in this fast moving world.

### I end my story with this poem:

> love flows within ourselves,
> if we choose to find it,
> heal ourselves
> and grow deeply
> within.

## *Additional Thoughts*

As my spiritual mentor, Laura, says, "The spiritual growth you will find is infinite—endless." And as it has been some months since she has said these very words to my face, I would agree. I am walking into a beautiful field and I have no idea how far the field continues, surrounded by wildlowers with the sun looking down at me—no matter where I go. Sensitive individuals can either learn to embrace themselves for who they are—and where that path leads to; or, they can continue trying to be somewhere else, trying to fit a mold that will never house and feed them properly—and could very possibly destroy them. It is quite simple indeed—in every moment, sensitive individuals must learn to love themselves for everything they feel—no matter what anyone else says.

When an Indigo Child firmly learns to love themselves every moment, he or she will most likely find that they become quite comfortable in their own skin. They may induldge in spending time with themselves—writing poetry for long hours, whispering to the trees on a long, beautiful day, or whatever else may fill an Indigo Child's heart. As an Indigo Child encounters this wonderful heart-space, I encourage these people to also remember the world and to not lose contact with where the world is. Remember, that as sensitive people, we do feel differently and look at the world differently; we must not lose contact with the real world and how we are able to help the people in the real world (who could be suffering).

It is said that when an individual spends extraordinary time with themselves, it is almost a greater call than this; yes, Indigo Children must learn to love themsleves. Furthermore, by continuing to spend time with one's self, one is almost seeking to create a loving, renewing connection with many people on the surface of the Earth. It can be challenging to find, create, and maintain this kind of connection on the Earth—during these times. Recognizing when one spends much time alone is an important step in spiritual growth. Self-discovery is important, but if one is stable and strong and flowing with love within—it is time to share this gift with others! It can be a fearful challenge for an Indigo Child, but it is a wonderful beautiful opportunity.

When an Indigo Child is radiating with love inside themselves and full of creativity (however it may manifest), this often a sign that an Indigo Child is strong within and ready to share his or her gift with the world! Whatever his or her gift may be! This is a gift that every Indigo Child must discover within himself; no book or map can guide you quite as well as the heart and mind that God gave you.

It is a beautiful journey that will unfold with everyday you breathe and thrive on this beautiful Earth.